Contents

Introduction

It's no good being clever if you can't understand and manage your emotions and get on with other people!

Emotional intelligence is now believed to be the most important sort of intelligence, and it involves us in:

- looking for verbal and non-verbal signs of different emotions and being able to name them

- thinking, talking about and responding to emotions

- knowing that different people respond in different ways and understanding why people feel the way they do

- learning how to manage our own emotions and respond appropriately to the emotions of others.

These skills are now acknowledged to be so important that they are central to early years practice across the world. Young children are directly and immediately influenced by their emotions, but as they have not yet learned how to understand and manage them, part of the job of parents, carers and early years practitioners is to explore these emotions with them. Emotional development covers many facets of growing up: how we feel, how we react to others, how we understand facial expressions, empathise and sympathise, and how we control our feelings, emotions and behaviours.

Personal, Social and Emotional Development (PSED) is the emotional intelligence thread that runs through everything practitioners do, and success in this area is a sign of high quality practice. However, planning for PSED is complex, and because it needs to permeate every area of the curriculum and every place in your setting, it is also at risk of not being planned at all!

The activities in this book have all been planned for you to use with small or larger groups, and with older children they can be offered to whole classes, particularly where there is additional adult help.

Short starter sessions are often useful when introducing new topics or discussing the daily events of your setting, and that is what you will find in this book: 50 ideas for starters taking form 10 - 20 minutes, with ideas for follow up that the children can manage independently or with a little adult help. Each activity is supported by stories that can extend your starter session into your work in Communication and Language and Literacy.

fantastic ideas for
exploring emotions

SALLY AND PHILL FEATHERSTONE

Published 2013 by Featherstone Education
Bloomsbury Publishing plc
50 Bedford Square, London, WC1B 3DP
www.bloomsbury.com

ISBN 978-1-4081-7979-6

Text © Sally and Phill Featherstone 2013
Design © Lynda Murray
Photographs © Sally Featherstone, © Shutterstock

Printed and bound in China by C&C Offset Printing Co. Ltd, Shenzen, Guangdong

This book is produced using paper that is made from wood grown in
managed, sustainable forests. It is natural, renewable and recyclable.
The logging and manufacturing processes conform to the environmental
regulations of the country of origin.

10 9 8 7 6 5 4 3 2 1

To see our full range of titles visit **www.bloomsbury.com**

Acknowledgements
Photographs with kind permission of London Early Years Foundation/Emli Bendixen,
and Acorn Childcare Ltd.

We have researched over 100 books, recommended for their contribution to emotional intelligence. Some are old favourites, which you will already know well, others may be new to you.

When planning for these activities, it is important to keep your focus on the feelings and emotions you want to explore, and to help you maintain this focus, we have separated the preparation of the resources from the activity with the children. By preparing some of the resources before the session it will give you and the children time during the shared session to concentrate fully on exploring feelings and emotions.

Resources

You will already have most of the resources you need for the activities in this book. However, you may want to beg, borrow, make or buy these, which will be very useful for embedding the activities into children's daily experiences.

- Feelings cards: make them yourself on small cards with simple line drawings of expressions.

- Puppets: one or two people puppets or empathy dolls. These characters are useful for discussing emotions and recreating situations.

- Photos of the children in your group: try to get several different pictures of each child, with different expressions. Print them and stick them on pieces of card about 10 x 15 cm.

- Storybooks: there are 100 suggested titles in this book - two on each page, and all recommended by practitioners, parents and others who work with children.

Skin allergy alert

Some detergents and soaps can cause skin reactions. Always be mindful of potential skin allergies when letting children mix anything with their hands and always provide lots of facilities to wash materials off after they have been in contact with the skin. Watch out for this symbol on the relevant pages.

Food allergy alert

When using food stuffs to enhance your outdoor play opportunties always be mindful of potential food allergies. We have used this symbol on the relevant pages.

The feelings beat
Naming feelings

What you need:

- A drum or tabor for you

Preparation:

- Make a list of all the names for emotions that you think are appropriate for your group, such as: happy, sad, angry, excited, cross, lonely, fidgety, silly, interested, frightened, jealous, selfish, peaceful, sleepy, mad, calm, surprised, lucky, pleased, brave, proud.

What to do:

1. Gather the children in a circle. Put the drum on the floor beside you.

2. Explain that you are going to play a clapping game about feelings. Say, 'I feel happy' then clap the beat of the words. Do this again with the children joining in.

3. Now pick up the drum and use this to make the beat as you say 'I feel...'. Practise together.

4. Encourage the children to make their faces match the expression as you say it. Mix the words up, and repeat some as they expand their vocabulary of feeling words.

5. Now ask the children to stand up and move in an appropriate way as they clap and move around the room.

6. At the end of the activity, pass a smile or a handshake around the circle.

Taking it forward

- Play this game in the hall, or outside.

- Use a wide range of feeling words as you talk with the children about everyday events.

What's in it for the children?

This activity gives children practice in learning the names for emotions.

A story or two

I Feel Frightened (Your Emotions series) by Brian Moses (Wayland)

I Feel Jealous (Your Emotions series) by Brian Moses (Wayland)

Hello, how are you?

Naming emotions, through greetings

What you need:

- A shaker or other sound maker

What to do:

1. Gather the children in a circle.

2. Explain that you are going to learn a new game called 'Hello'.

3. Turn to the child next to you and say 'Hello (name)'. The other child should say 'Hello' in return.

4. This child turns to the next child and repeats the greeting.

5. Keep going around the circle until the greeting comes back to you.

6. Now get the children to stand up and spread out.

7. When you say 'Go' the children walk about anywhere in the room as you shake the shaker. When you say 'Stop' they shake hands with someone near them and say 'Hello (name)'. The other child says 'Hello (name)'.

8. Shake the shaker again and continue.

9. Keep going, until the children have shaken several hands.

10. Now shake the shaker, stop and say 'Walk back to the circle'.

11. When the children are settled, thank them for how well they remembered everyone's name.

Taking it forward

- Play this game outside or in the hall – it's sometimes harder in a bigger space.

- Use the game as a way of taking the register.

What's in it for the children?

This activity gives children practice in acknowledging others.

A story or two

The Name Jar by Yangsook Choi (Dragonfly)

Liam Says Hi by Jane Whelen Banks (Jessica Kingsley)

Feel it in your feet!
Recognising and expressing emotions

What you need:

- Two simple sound makers: a drum, tambourine, shaker, bells, rain stick etc
- A big space, such as the carpet or the hall: you could also play this game outside in dry weather

Preparation:

- Remind yourself of the different emotions that are familiar to the children. You could make yourself a small 'crib card' for your pocket.

Taking it forward

- Offer a box of different shoes so they can play the game independently.

- Sing 'If you're wearing angry shoes you need to stamp,' to the tune of 'If You're Happy and You Know it…'.

What's in it for the children?

This activity gives children practice in recognising how different emotions feel.

A story or two

All Kinds of Feelings by Emma Brownjohn (Tango Books)

Where my Wellies Take Me by Michael Morpurgo (Templar Publishing)

What to do:

1. Before you start, tell the children that you are going to play 'Put on your feeling shoes'.

2. They need to lie down on the floor and pretend to be asleep.

3. You will wake them up by making one of the sounds, and telling them which imaginary shoes to put on: such as angry shoes, happy shoes, scared shoes, tired shoes and so on.

4. The children must wake up and put on the feelings shoes. Once they have their shoes on they can move around the space showing you how they are feeling: angry stamping, scared creeping, shy tiptoeing and so on.

5. Start the game with a feeling that is easy for them to show, such as 'Put on your angry shoes'.

6. Continue with the game until the children have tried on several pairs of shoes.

7. Now ask them to sit down while some volunteers show the group their favourite shoes.

8. Talk about how the shoes made them feel and move, ask the group how they could tell what sort of shoes they were.

Pleased to see you
Showing how you feel

What you need:

- The home corner door, or the door to your room
- Feelings face cards
- For younger children, you may need an additional adult

Preparation:

- Find or make some feelings face cards: small cards with simple line drawings of faces on them such as happy, sad, cross, upset, scared and tired.

Taking it forward

- Play the same game whenever you have a new role-play area such as a shop or baby clinic, so children can practise making welcoming faces.

- Stick a smiling face on the inside of the door to your room, at child height, as a reminder to greet visitors and parents with a smile.

What's in it for the children?

This activity gives children practice in greeting people with a smile.

A story or two

Knock, Knock, Who's There? by Sally Grindley (Puffin)

Knock, Knock by David Bedford (Little Hare)

What to do:

1. Sit together where you can all see the home corner door.

2. Show the children the feelings face cards, and hold each one up in turn, saying 'How do you think this person is feeling?'

3. Give the children some time to look at the pictures and name the feeling.

4. Now tell them you are going to play 'Knock on the door'. This is how you play: one child will take the feeling face cards, go inside the home corner and shut the door. They will then choose one feeling face card, but not tell anyone what it is.

5. Ask a volunteer to do this, they may need an adult to help them.

6. The other children say 'Knock, knock, knock at the door. Open up and show us more!'

7. The person inside the home corner opens the door showing their face with the appropriate expression on their chosen card. The rest of the children guess how they are feeling. Now choose another volunteer.

8. When you have played the game a few times, with different children, ask the group how the expression of the person in the doorway makes them feel.

9. Remind them how nice it is to be greeted with a smile.

Roll a smile

Making eye contact

What you need:

- A big, soft ball, such as a beach ball, or lightweight football

What to do:

1. Gather the children in a circle.
2. Explain that you are going to play a game called 'Roll a smile'.
3. Practise smiling, by sending a smile round the circle, passing the ball as you smile at your neighbour.
4. Now explain that you are going to roll the ball across the circle to another person. First you look at them, then smile, then roll the ball.
5. Start the ball rolling yourself, by making eye contact with a child, smiling and rolling the ball.
6. This child rolls the ball to another, and so on. Try to make sure everyone gets a turn.
7. Finish the game by passing a congratulations handshake or a 'high five' round the circle.

Taking it forward

- Play this game outside, rolling or tossing a ball, a beanbag, or even a pair of socks.
- Encourage children to make and maintain eye contact when they are communicating with others.

What's in it for the children?

This activity gives children practice in looking at other people's faces and making eye contact.

A story or two

Kipper's Beach Ball by Mick Inkpen (Hodder)

The Little Book of Circle Time by Dawn Roper (Featherstone)

Make a face
Recognising and naming emotions

What you need:

- Space for circle time
- A teddy or other toy

Preparation:

- Practise exaggerating your facial expressions, to help children learn to recognise emotions in other people.

Taking it forward

- Make some simple 'feelings face' cards. Use them to play 'Pairs', putting the cards face down and letting the children take turns to turn over two at a time to find matching emotions.

- Use the same cards for a sorting discussion: which faces are happy, sad or angry? How can you tell?

What's in it for the children?

This activity gives children practice in recognising and copying simple expressions of emotions.

A story or two

Funny Face by Nicola Smee (Bloomsbury)

Make a Face by Allan Ahlberg (Walker Books)

What to do:

1. Gather the children in a circle.

2. Choose a name for the teddy or toy, by asking the children for suggestions.

3. Tell the children you are going to learn another game about feelings. Explain that this time they will need to watch each other carefully, as you are going to pass the feeling and the toy all the way round the circle from one person to another.

4. Concentrate on just a few simple emotions such as happy, sad or scared.

5. Say the emotion and make the face yourself first, exaggerating your expression so everyone can see what you are doing. Turn to the child next to you and pass the toy and the emotion to them. They make the face and pass it on to the next child. (Don't worry if some children find it difficult to convey the emotion and the toy together! Just keep the game going.)

6. When the toy gets back to you, praise the children for their work and choose another feeling to send round. Remind the children to look at their friends' faces as they pass the toy.

7. Repeat the game just two or three times.

We are all friends

Listening to and thinking about others

What you need:

- A photograph of the face of each child in the group

Preparation:

- If you haven't got photos of each child, take some and print them.

Taking it forward

- Prepare lots of small versions of their photos (postage stamp size) and copies of all the children's names, so they can write letters and cards to each other.

- Make a 'Who is this?' photo book in a slip photo album.

What's in it for the children?

This activity gives children practice in acknowledging others.

A story or two

Night Monkey, Day Monkey by Julia Donaldson (Egmont Books)

Q Pootle 5 by Nick Butterworth (HarperCollins)

What to do:

1. Sit in a circle. Explain that you are going to talk about each other.

2. Use this 'quick swapping' activity so the children are not necessarily sitting next to their best friend. Say 'If you are wearing shoes with laces, stand up and swap places with someone else who is wearing shoes with laces. Now if you have curly hair, stand up and swap. If you have brown eyes, stand up and swap.' This should make sure the children are well mixed!

3. Now, starting with the child next to you, get the children to turn so they are in pairs.

4. Spread the photos on the floor and ask them to fetch their own photo.

5. Give the children some time to look at their own photo, and their partner's photo.

6. Start yourself and then take turns round the circle. Hold up your photo and say, 'I'm Mrs Layton and I like telling stories'. Turn to the child next to you so they can introduce themselves.

7. When all the children have introduced themselves, get the partners to swap photos and introduce each other: 'This is Arianne and she likes painting.'

8. Praise the children for remembering information and thinking about other people.

Cut it out

Listening to and thinking about others

What you need:

- **Some pictures showing faces expressing emotions** (cut from magazines or catalogues)
- **A flat space, where you can lay out the pictures**

Preparation:

- Cut out some pictures of faces from magazines and newspapers, showing different emotions. You need two or three pictures for each emotion.

What to do:

1. Gather the children in a circle.
2. Explain that you have some pictures of faces that show how people feel.
3. Spread out the pictures in the centre of the circle, and as you put each photo down say, 'How do you think this person is feeling?'
4. Give the children some time to look at the pictures and talk about them to a 'talking partner'.
5. Invite one of the pairs to choose a picture and talk to the rest of the children about how the person is feeling. How can they tell?
6. Ask all the children if they can make their face show the same feeling.
7. Invite other children to choose a picture to talk about.
8. Praise the children for how carefully they have looked at feelings.

Taking it forward

- Make the photos available so the children can talk about them afterwards with their friends.
- Suggest that children could add to the collection by bringing pictures from home.

What's in it for the children?

This activity gives children practice in recognising and describing the facial features of emotions.

A story or two

Sometimes I Feel Sunny by Gillian Shields (Picture Corgi)

Bridget Fidget by Joe Berger (Puffin)

The blanket of feelings

Recognising and naming emotions

What you need:

- **A puppet or doll to 'tell' the story** (give this character a name, and use it for the story)

What to do:

1. Gather the children in a circle.

2. Introduce the character in the story. Say 'This is (Ellie), and our story today is about her.' Put the puppet or doll on a chair beside you as you tell the story, changing the name if you need to:

One day Ellie was riding her bike on the path near her house. She was so busy telling herself a story that she forgot to look where she was going, and she rode right out into the road.

What do you think happened next? (pause for ideas)

There was a big crash, and a car had knocked Ellie off her bike. She was lying in the road and she wasn't moving. Her legs hurt really badly, and she had bumped her head on the road.

Lots of people came running over when they heard the crash. One of them phoned for the ambulance. Her mum came running too.

The ambulance driver looked at Ellie and said, 'I think you need to come to the hospital.' Ellie's mum went with her in the ambulance.

When they got to the hospital, the doctor said she must stay there until she was better. It took a long time for Ellie's legs to get better. She had to sit in a wheelchair, and do exercises to strengthen her muscles. The exercises hurt her, and sometimes she was very sad and lonely.

When Ellie's friends at school heard about the accident, they talked about what they could do to cheer her up. Some of her friends made cards to send her, some drew pictures. Her best friend Max came to see her in the hospital. He brought all the cards and pictures and the nurses put them up round Ellie's bed. Ellie was very happy to see that her friends still thought about her. But Ellie still felt lonely, especially in the night, when her mum was asleep, and her legs hurt her.

When she heard about this, Ellie's teacher had an idea. She brought a blanket into school, and asked the children if they would like to make a feelings blanket for Ellie. All the children said 'Yes!'

So the children drew lots of pictures of their faces on bits of fabric. Some drew happy faces to cheer Ellie up, some drew sad faces so Ellie knew they were missing her. Some drew angry faces, and these children said they were angry that Ellie had been hurt. Some of them drew silly faces to stop Ellie feeling scared in the night.

When they had finished, their teacher helped them to stick all the fabric pictures onto the blanket. It looked great!

Ellie's mum took the blanket to the hospital and put it on Ellie's bed, where it kept her company until she was better. Ellie sent a very happy photo to thank her friends for their kind present, and the doctor said it really helped her to get well again.

3. How do the children think Ellie felt when she saw the feelings blanket her friends had made?

4. Ask any children who have been in hospital to share their experiences and feelings.

Taking it forward

- Make a real feelings blanket by asking the children to draw feelings faces on a sheet or other big piece of fabric. Tape the fabric down on the floor or a table and use felt pens or fabric crayons to draw the faces directly onto the sheet. Hang the blanket on the wall or put it in your quiet area for the children to use.

What's in it for the children?

This activity gives children practice in empathising.

A story or two

The Red Woollen Blanket by Bob Graham (Walker Books)

Going to the Hospital by Anna Civardi (Usborne)

50 fantastic ideas for exploring emotions

How are you feeling today?

Expressing feelings

What you need:

- A big sheet of card, a mobile pin board or a flipchart
- Name cards for each child and each adult in the group
- Sticky tack or double-sided tape, felt pens

Preparation:

- Prepare a registration board like this on paper, card or a flipchart:

  How are you feeling today?

Taking it forward

- If a child is feeling distressed or angry when they arrive, take time to be with them, or make sure they have a friend to look after them.

- Download some free emoticons from Google and use these to help the children to discuss how they feel.

What's in it for the children?

This activity gives children practice in recognising their own emotions and how they might change over time.

A story or two

Alexander and the Terrible, Horrible, No Good, Very Bad Day by Judith Viorst (Atheneum Books)

The Good Mood Hunt by Hiawyn Oram (Oxford University Press)

What to do:

1. Gather the children in a circle.

2. Explain that you are going to have a different sort of register. The register will show how everyone is feeling.

3. Now demonstrate, using your own name, saying 'This is how I am feeling today'. Stick your name in the first column, then draw a 'feeling face' in the next column, explaining why you felt this way. (It's OK to put a sad or grumpy face if that's what you really feel!)

4. Now invite one of the children to come and find their name, stick it under yours, and draw how they are feeling.

5. When all the children understand how to register, show the children where the register will be kept, so they can add their own names and feelings faces.

6. As children come into your setting on the following days, stand near the registration board to remind them to think about how they are feeling.

High five!
Recognising and expressing emotions

What you need:

- A felt pen for each pair of children

Preparation:

- Secretly draw a simple smiling face on the palm of one hand and a sad face on the palm of the other hand. You may need some help, at least with one of these!

Taking it forward

- Use 'high five' faces when you read or tell stories.

- Draw different expressions on each finger. Now play 'Simon says' with these faces: Simon says 'sad', 'happy', 'scared' and so on and the children must hold up the appropriate finger.

What's in it for the children?

This activity gives children practice in recognising simple emotions and choosing the one they feel.

A story or two

Hands Are Not For Hitting by Martine Agassi (A&C Black)

My Hands by Aliki (HarperCollins)

What to do:

1. Gather the children in a circle.

2. Explain that you are going to play the 'High five' feelings game.

3. Get the children to choose a friend to work with.

4. Now show the children your hands and explain that today you have a sad hand and a happy hand. Hold up each one as you talk.

5. Explain that they need to get ready for the game by helping their friend to draw a happy face on one of their hands and a sad face on the other.

6. Now everyone sits with their hands closed and on their knees.

7. You begin the game by saying 'How does this make you feel? A puppy is hungry. High five the hand that shows how you feel about that'. Hold up your sad hand in a 'high five'.

8. Continue with other short situations: 'It's your birthday', 'You lose your glove', 'You see a smiling baby', 'You miss your mum', 'You find a spider','You bang your knee'.

9. Invite some children to tell their own happy/sad stories for others to respond to.

10. Finish the session by high five-ing smiling face hands with your neighbour: passing a smile round the circle.

I remember when

Recognising achievements

What you need:

- A large piece of paper
- A space for the paper on the floor or a flipchart stand
- Felt pens
- Sticky notes

Taking it forward

- Offer the children some pictures cut from baby catalogues or magazines to make collages of the things babies need.

- Ask children to bring their own pictures of themselves as babies. Make a display by taking photos of the children to display alongside their baby pictures.

What's in it for the children?

This activity reminds children how they have grown and what they can now do, to build their self-esteem.

A story or two

The Elephant and the Bad Baby by Elfrida Vipont (Puffin)

The Baby Who Wouldn't Go To Bed by Helen Cooper (Corgi)

What to do:

1. Gather the children in a circle where they can all see the paper.

2. Explain that you are going to talk about being grown up.

3. Ask the children what 'grown up' means: 'Are you grown up?', 'Is a baby grown up?', 'Is a teenager grown up?'.

4. Give the children some time to speak to a talk partner or to think about what it means, then choose some volunteers to talk.

5. Talk about how they are more grown up than babies, but not as grown up as adults.

6. Draw three circles on the paper and label the first 'What babies can do', the second 'What we can do', and the third 'What mums and dads can do'.

7. Invite the children to suggest what babies can do, what children can do and what adults can do. Draw or write their responses on sticky notes and stick them in the appropriate circle.

8. Look at the differences between the baby circle, the child circle and the grown up circle. Emphasise the positives about growing up.

Animal antics
Recognising and naming characteristics

What to do:

1. Gather the children in a circle.

2. Help them to remember all the 'feelings' names they now know: happy, sad, cheerful, angry, scared, cross, worried, upset, shy, excited. You could add more ideas, particularly for older children: mad, proud, cheerful, daring, selfish, loving, friendly.

3. Show the children the animals you have collected and say that you are going to give them all new names.

4. Hold up one of the animals or puppets and make sure the children agree on the name of the animal.

5. Now say 'Listen to his name – he is a frog – we could call him Friendly Frog. How do you think Friendly Frog got his name?'

6. Choose a volunteer to tell Friendly Frog's story.

7. Now let this child choose another animal, and go through the same process.

8. Get the children to sit with a friend and choose an animal from your basket or box, and try to find a name for it. Older children could also make up a story about why the animal has this name.

9. If you have another adult with you, ask them to write down the children's ideas, so you don't forget.

Taking it forward

- Take a photo of each animal with the pair of children, and make a display of the photos.

- Try the same idea with the children's own names; Loving Laura, Helpful Henry, Enthusiastic Emma and so on. Make sure the names are positive, and cannot be used to tease or annoy the individual child.

What's in it for the children?

This activity gives children practice in naming emotions and thinking about what they mean.

A story or two

Angry Arthur by Hiawyn Oram (Andersen)

Clumsy Crab by Ruth Galloway (Little Tiger Press)

Sort us out!

Naming and emotions

What you need:

- Photos of the children in your group
- Some hoops or circles of string (for sorting)
- Small cards with simple faces (happy/sad/excited/scared/angry) **drawn in black felt pen**

Preparation:

- Take some photos of the children's faces. Take at least two photos of each child. Ask a child or another adult to take photos of you too!
- Print the photos so the face is about life size. Laminate them, or stick them onto card, they will be useful for other games too.

Taking it forward

- Print some small versions of the photos. Use these for independent games of sorting.
- Use the photos on the 'How are you feeling today?' board for a change (see page 16).

What's in it for the children?

This activity gives children practice in recognising emotions from their own and others' facial expressions.

A story or two

Have You Filled a Bucket Today? by Merrill Lundgren (Nelson Publishing)

Albert Le Blanc by Nick Butterworth (HarperCollins)

What to do:

1. Gather the children in a circle.
2. Put the photos on the carpet. Give the children time to look at each one and talk to each other about them.
3. Now invite one child to pick up their own photos and hold them in front of their face, one at a time, so everyone has time to look.
4. Talk about how the photos make the child look different.
5. Now let all the children do the same in talking pairs, each with their own photos.
6. Show the children the hoops or circles of string. Tell them that you want them to sort their photos as they return them to the carpet.
7. Put the circles on the carpet and put a feelings card in each one. Ask the children to put their pictures in the right circle.
8. Keep talking about the photos as the children put them in the circles.

50 fantastic ideas for exploring emotions

When the wind blew

Recognising the effect of emotions on the body

What you need:

- A shaker or a tambourine
- A flat space, such as the carpet, the hall or a dry day outside

Preparation:

- Remind yourself of the 'old wives' tale that when the wind changes direction, anyone making a funny, angry or silly face will stay like it forever.

Taking it forward

- Tell a story about the wind changing. *When the Wind Changed* (see below) is about a boy who made faces and the wind did change!

- Go outside on a windy day and see how it makes you feel. Take some ribbon sticks and run in the wind. Talk about how the wind can make you feel excited and fidgety.

What's in it for the children?

This activity gives children practice in recognising the physical features of emotions.

A story or two

If the Wind Changes by Steve Smallman (QED publishing)

When the Wind Changed by Ruth Park (Angus and Robertson

What to do:

1. Sit together on the carpet so you can explain this game.

2. Tell the children about the old story of what happens when the wind changes direction. Make sure they understand that the tale is not true, only you can make your face stay in one expression.

3. Explain that your game is a bit different. In your game, the shaker is the wind, and the wind can make feelings go away. You will say a feeling, and the children will make the face. Gradually the wind will start to blow, and when it is really blowing, you will say 'Feeling go!'.

4. Have a practice. Say a feeling word, and the children make the face. Gradually make the shaker sound louder and louder. Then say 'Feeling go!'.

5. Say another feeling, and this time, the children can move around to express the feeling, using their whole bodies.

6. Control the game with the shaker, and when you think the children have explored that emotion, say again 'Feeling go!'.

7. Praise the children's work in expressing emotions through their bodies and faces.

Making faces for Kim

Naming and drawing emotions

What you need:

- A whiteboard for each child
- Dry-wipe pens
- Board erasers or kitchen towels
- A human puppet or doll

What to do:

1. Gather the children in a circle.
2. Introduce the puppet or doll. We have called the character Kim, you could use another name.
3. Explain the game to the children. You are going to tell a story about Kim. You will stop sometimes and ask them to draw a face on their whiteboard to show how they think Kim felt at this part of the story.
4. Give each child a whiteboard, pen and eraser.
5. Ask for volunteers to name a feeling for the others to draw. Hold up your drawings for others to see. Extend the range if you need to by suggesting brave, nervous, excited and so on.
6. Clean the boards.

Taking it forward

- Make some photo stories using the puppet from the story. Use simple storylines about your setting and the things that happen there.
- When children talk about their own experiences in group time, try using a whiteboard to record their emotions as they tell the story.

What's in it for the children?

This activity gives children practice in recognising the facial features of emotions.

A story or two

On the Way Home by Jill Murphy (Macmillan)

Peace at Last by Jill Murphy (Macmillan)

7. Now begin the story:

One day Kim went to school. Kim loved school and he was looking forward to playing with Sandy. (Stop for the children to draw the face, and then hold up their boards for you to see.)

On the way to school, Kim went past the house where the big black dog lived. (Stop for another feeling face. You may be able to talk about different faces here, as some children will like dogs, others won't.)

Kim said goodbye to the dog and went round the corner, and there was Sandy, waiting for him with a big smile on her face. (Stop.)

Kim and Sandy hung up their coats and went into their room. Their teacher wasn't there! There was a new teacher that they had never seen before. (Stop for drawing and comments.)

Kim and Sandy sat down on the carpet. The new teacher asked them questions, and when she looked at Kim, he didn't want to answer. (Stop.)

Kim wished it was time to go home. (Stop.)

Sandy said 'Don't be sad, Kim, let's go and play with the building bricks. They went off to play and Kim felt better. (Stop.)

The new teacher was really kind and she let them play with her bag of finger puppets at story time. So when Kim's mum came to fetch him, he was feeling much better, and his face looked like this. (Stop.)

8. Praise the children for their work in making the story faces.

9. Ask them if they have ever felt like Kim did.

Copy cat!

Understanding facial expressions

What you need:

- **Some pictures showing faces expressing emotions** (cut from magazines or catalogues)

- **A flat space, such as the carpet**

Taking it forward

- Use positive reinforcement and sing the song when you are all happy, proud and successful.

- Play 'Feelings statues' where the children dance or move around and when a caller calls out a feeling, they freeze in that emotion, using face and body to express the feeling.

What's in it for the children?

This activity gives children practice in recognising the external evidence of inner emotions.

A story or two

I Feel Angry (Your Emotions series) by Brian Moses (Wayland)

I Feel Sad (Your Emotions series) by Brian Moses (Wayland)

What to do:

1. Gather the children in a circle.

2. Teach the children this song - to the tune of 'The Wheels on the Bus'.

   The Copy Cat Song

   The look on my face will show you all
   Show you all, show you all.
   The look on my face will show you all
   How I feel inside.

   Copy my face and you will see,
   You will see, you will see.
   Copy my face and you will see
   How I feel inside.

3. Practise the song a few times.

4. Now show the children one of your pictures that shows a very strong emotion. As they look at the picture, sing the song again.

5. Ask the children 'How do you think this person is feeling? Can you copy this feelings face?'.

6. Give the children time to look at the picture and copy the expression. Say altogether: 'I'm happy!' (or whatever the emotion is in the picture).

7. Choose another picture, sing the song and make the new face.

8. Invite some children to choose a picture, leading the singing of the song as they do. This time, as they finish the song, add the last line: 'I'm proud!'.

Fish a feeling
Understanding emotions through a story

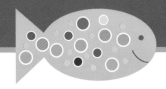

What you need:

- A copy of *The Rainbow Fish* by Marcus Pfister (North-South Books)
- A piece of shiny fabric
- Some big sequins or shiny buttons

Preparation:

- Read the story so you are familiar with what happens.
- Drape a chair with the shiny fabric, scatter some big sequins on the fabric, and put the book on the chair just before the session. If the children watch you preparing, they will feel more involved and excited!

Taking it forward

- Leave the book where the children can reread it and replay the story themselves.
- Make pictures and collages of the Rainbow Fish with captions and words to describe the feelings in the story.

What's in it for the children?

This activity gives children practice in recognising emotions in stories.

A story or two

How to be a Friend by Laurene Krasny Brown (Little, Brown)

Elmer by David McKee (Andersen)

What to do:

1. Gather the children in a circle.

2. You could include your Feelings Panda (page 26) or any character that you use for circle time or PSED sessions.

3. Tell the children that the story you are about to read to them is about feelings, so they need to think as well as listen.

4. Read the storybook through without stopping.

5. Talk with the children about the emotions in the story: Can they remember the word for the way the Rainbow Fish behaved at the beginning? What does 'proud' mean? How did the little fish feel when the Rainbow Fish wouldn't give him a shiny scale?

6. Can they make the faces for someone who is proud?

7. How did the octopus make the Rainbow Fish change his mind?

8. When you have discussed these aspects, you could act out the story.

9. Read the storybook through again slowly, without stopping as the children act it out.

Don't upset the panda!

Recognising and naming expressions

What you need:

- Two pieces of stiff card, about A3 size
- Tape
- Felt pens
- Scissors

Preparation:

- Cut an oval hole in the first piece of card to make the face of the panda (see diagram 1). Add ears and draw paws on the card to make the panda look as if he is sitting.

- Put the second piece of card underneath the first piece and draw in pencil round the face hole three or four times across the card. Use felt pens to draw a different expression in each face circle: happy and smiling, sad, angry, scared, fierce, brave etc (see diagram 2).

- Join the short ends of the first card together to make a cylinder, and fasten with tape so it will stand up.

- Now join the ends of the second cylinder, making it a bit smaller than the first one so it will fit inside. Check that the inner cylinder will slide round so the faces show through the hole in the outer tube (see diagram 3).

What to do:

1. Gather the children in a circle.

2. Explain that you have made a 'Feelings Panda', and he hasn't got a name. Use the children's suggestions to choose a name.

3. Show the children how the panda works by sliding the cylinder round to reveal each of the faces.

4. As you change the panda's expression, ask the children to suggest what s/he is feeling, and if they can guess why.

5. Use the panda for some of the games you have learned so far, and make her/him a permanent feature of your setting by giving him a place to sit and watch the children.

6. Tell or read a story about panda's day or use him to reflect emotions within the group or individual children's experiences.

7. Your panda could be used to reflect the feelings in your group: happy when the sun is shining, cross when something gets broken or lost.

Taking it forward

- Tell the story of *Albert Le Blanc* by Nick Butterworth (HarperCollins), using the panda to show his feelings.

- Sing The Copy Cat Song (page 24) and turn the panda's face to show different feelings.

What's in it for the children?

This activity gives children practice in linking emotional expressions with events.

A story or two

Little Panda by Renata Liwska (Houghton Mifflin/Harcourt)

I'm Feeling Angry by Lisa Regan (Featherstone)

What's in a name?

Naming characteristics

What you need:

- Some pictures of children cut out from magazines, catalogues, or illustrations from old or damaged books

Preparation:

- Look through your pictures and prepare yourself by giving some of the children descriptive names.

- Here are some examples, you will probably be able to think of more: Smiling Sam, Nervous Nancy, Angry Adam, Lonely Len, Brave Beena, Friendly Fergus, Adventurous Amy, Charming Charlie.

What to do:

1. Gather the children in a circle.

2. Tell them you are going to introduce them to some new children by saying their names and showing a photo of them.

3. Hold up the first photo and say the name you have given to this child, such as Smiling Sam.

4. Give the children some time to look at the picture. Can they make their face like Smiling Sam's?

5. Ask why the child has this name. What would Smiling Sam be like if he came to your setting? What would he do? Would you like to be his friend?

6. Offer some volunteers a chance to choose a photo and discuss these.

7. Now ask the children to think about their own name and see if they can make a new name for themselves by adding another word that describes what they are like.

8. Praise any attempts and suggest some ideas for names.

Taking it forward

- Stick the photos in a blank book and invite the children to write the names or draw pictures of their own faces.

- Make a display of photos of the children in your group with their names and talents.

What's in it for the children?

This activity gives children practice in understanding some simple words for personal characteristics.

A story or two

The Very Helpful Hedgehog by Rosie Wellesley (Pavilion Children's Books)

One Snowy Night by Nick Butterworth (HarperCollins)

The Happy Book

Understanding and describing being happy

What you need:

- A big blank book
- A thick marker
- Magazines and catalogues
- Glue sticks

Preparation:

- Make or get a suitable blank book to make a 'Happy book'.
- Collect some magazines, holiday brochures and catalogues.

What to do:

1. Gather the children in a circle.
2. Ask the children what makes them happy, and let them discuss this with a talk partner before sharing some ideas across the group.
3. Explain that you are going to make a book together about all the things that make people happy, and first you need to make the cover: a cover filled with happiness!
4. Put some magazines, brochures and catalogues in the middle of the group, and ask the children to look for happy faces in the adverts and pictures. When they find one, they can carefully tear it out and bring it to stick on the cover of the book. If you have a big group, you may need to offer a container for pictures and stick them on later. The aim of the activity is to recognise and select happy faces, not to practise cutting out!
5. As the children bring their faces, ask them why they think the person is happy.
6. While you all work you could sing happy songs such as, 'If You're Happy and You Know It…' or 'You are My Sunshine'.

Taking it forward

- Put the Happy Book on a table and encourage the children to contribute photos, drawings and other images of happy times for all of you: outings, parties, visitors, children's achievements.
- Suggest that children could add to the Happy Book with pictures from home.

What's in it for the children?

This activity gives children practice in recognising the things that make them happy.

A story or two

If You're Happy and You Know It by Jan Ormerod (Oxford University Press)

The Happy Hedgehog Band by Martin Waddell (Walker Books)

Different is good!

Looking at differences and what is unique about individuals

What you need:

- A big selection of small world or toy elephants
- The picture book *Elmer* by David McKee (Anderson).
- Bag

Preparation:

- Practise the story and how you will use the characters.
- Put the book and the elephants in a bag.
- If you have an Elmer toy, add it to the bag, if you haven't, you could copy the picture from the book cover and laminate it so it stands up.

Taking it forward

- Make zig-zag books of Elmer's story.
- Make a display about friends. Take photos of children and their friends, and display these with books about friendship.

What's in it for the children?

This activity gives children practice in acknowledging that everyone is different.

A story or two

Tell Me Something Happy Before I Go to Sleep by Joyce Dunbar (Corgi)

I Want a Friend by Tony Ross (HarperCollins

What to do:

1. Gather the children in a circle.
2. Say, 'Today we are thinking about friends, and I'm going to tell you a story about a time when things went wrong for some friends. This story is about elephants'.
3. Find out what they know about elephants: their colour, their size, what they eat and do, where they live. Do they live in groups? Do they have friends?
4. Now say, 'How can you tell if an elephant is happy? Do elephants smile? Do elephants feel sad? How can you tell?'
5. Take your elephants out of the bag and put them on the floor or a low table where the children can see them.
6. Say, 'Our story today is about an elephant who was happy, then sad, then happy again. Take Elmer from the bag and stand him next to the other elephants.
7. Take the book from the bag and read the story through without stopping.
8. Ask the children if they noticed when Elmer was happy, and when he was sad. As they think and talk, find the pictures in the book, or move the elephants around.

Ha! Ha! Ha!
Enjoying laughter

What you need:

- Catalogues, magazines and brochures
- A flat space, such as the carpet.

Preparation:

- Cut out some pictures of laughing faces – holiday brochures always have happy photos. Look for people of all types, ages and races.

Taking it forward

- Make a big sun on a display board and let the children add pictures of themselves with a short sentence, 'I am happy because…'.

- On a big sheet of card, make a collage of all the happy face photos. Paint all over the collage with dilute PVA glue. Use it for a book cover, display background or play mat.

What's in it for the children?

This activity gives children opportunities to see the effect of smiling on others and on themselves.

A story or two

Winnie's Jokes by Valerie Thomas (Oxford University Press)

Laughing Giraffe by Mwenye Hadithi (Hodder Children's Books)

What to do:

1. Gather the children in a circle with their talking partners.

2. Spread the photos out on the carpet and say, 'What do you notice about all these people?'

3. Give the children some time to look at the pictures and talk about them to each other.

4. Invite the children to offer ideas. Listen carefully: they may see things that you haven't noticed!

5. Now talk about why all the people are laughing. Can they think of a reason? How do we know they are happy?

6. Encourage them to pick up the pictures and talk about individuals: this baby is laughing because he's got his dinner; this girl is laughing because she is jumping in the pool.

7. Now ask the children to talk in pairs about what makes them laugh. Can they make each other laugh without touching them?

8. Pass a smile around the circle.

We've got talent
Taking pride in success

What you need:

- A whiteboard, flipchart or big piece of paper
- A reminder list, timetable or even your planning!
- Sticky notes

Preparation:

- Think back over the week, and remind yourself of all the things you have done and all the things the children have learned. You could jot things down as you go through the week so you don't forget anything or anyone.

Taking it forward

- Display the poster somewhere prominent and encourage the children to show their parents.
- Repeat this activity every few weeks, so children get used to acknowledging their own and others' achievements.

What's in it for the children?

This activity gives children practice in recognising and taking pride in their achievements.

A story or two

The Nativity Play by Nick Butterworth and Mick Inkpen (Hodder Children's Books)

Katie Morag and the Grand Concert by Mairi Hedderwick (Red Fox).

What to do:

1. Gather the children in a circle with their talking partners.

2. Say, 'Here we are at '*(Yellow Group's) Got Talent!*' Time to remember how clever we all are!'

3. Invite the children to think about all the great things they have done during the week. You may need to remind them by showing some photos or talking about special events.

4. Give the children some time to think and talk about them to each other. Invite some pairs of children to talk about something they remember. Encourage them to talk about other children as well as themselves.

5. As they tell you about the week, note the event or activity and the child's names on sticky notes and put them on the whiteboard, flipchart or paper. If you have two adults, one could talk with the children while the other writes the sticky notes.

6. When everyone has had a chance to contribute, add anything that they have missed, and make special mention of any children who deserve praise. Make this an event where everyone feels included.

7. Finally pass a high five around the circle.

I can do it! Yes I can!

Recognising success and achievement

What you need:

- A camera
- Space to move
- A turn-taking object, such as a shell or small soft toy

What to do:

1. Gather the children in a circle with their talk partners.

2. Explain that you want them to think hard about what they are good at and how they can show the group their skills. Let them talk to their partners about it first.

3. Now go round the group, passing the shell or toy, each child saying 'I can…'. If a child doesn't want to join in, move on.

4. Now let the children practise with their partner, taking turns to show each other their skill. They may need to fetch things from the room – be sensitive to this!

5. As they practise, you (or another adult) can take photos for a book or display.

6. End the activity with 'pass the hand shake' or 'pass the pat on the back' around the circle.

Taking it forward

- Print the photos and let the children make them into a book with their own captions.

- Make an 'I can' space on a low pin board for children's celebrations of their own achievements.

What's in it for the children?

This activity gives children practice in recognising their own unique skills and abilities.

A story or two

Yes We Can by Sam McBratney (Puffin)

I Can Do Maths Today by Dr Seuss (HarperCollins)

Please look after me!
Caring for others

What you need:

- **A soft toy that is new to the children** (try charity shops)
- **Some string**
- **A label**

Preparation:

- Write 'Please look after me, I am lost.' on the label and tie it round the toy's neck.
- Before the children arrive, leave the toy somewhere in the room or the outside area for the children to find.

What to do:

1. When someone finds the hidden toy, gather the children together.
2. Read the label and ask the children what they think they should do to look after the toy.
3. The children will have plenty of ideas, and the activity may take off without any help from you. If they do need help, ask them what the toy would need: somewhere to sleep, something to eat, a name, friends.
4. Some of the children will take to this activity with enthusiasm, and the toy may become the focus for them all day or even longer.
5. Remember to praise the children for their ideas.

Taking it forward

- Let the children take the toy home in turn, telling everyone about their adventures in the morning.
- Make up stories about where the toy came from and how it got to your setting.

What's in it for the children?

This activity gives children experience of looking after 'someone' else.

A story or two

This is the Bear by Sarah Hayes (Walker Books)

Where's My Teddy? by Jez Alborough (Walker Books)

Please look after me, I am lost.

Flip it!

Recognising and naming facial expressions

What you need:

- **Paper plates** (enough for half a plate for each member of the group, including adults)
- **A felt pen or fat crayon for each person**

Preparation:

- Cut the paper plates in half.

Taking it forward

- Keep the plates available to use during stories.

- Offer the children a mirror so they can see how their face changes as they turn their smile upside down.

What's in it for the children?

This activity gives children practice in recognising the different signals we give to show our emotions.

A story or two

Even My Ears are Smiling by Michael Rosen (Bloomsbury)

Tiger, Tiger is it True? by Byron Katie (Hay House)

What to do:

1. Gather the children in a circle.

2. Give each person a half plate and a pen.

3. Ask the children what their mouth looks like when they smile – practise and look at each other. Now explain that you want them to draw a big smile on their plate, big enough for everyone to see.

4. Give the children some time to draw a smile, helping any who find it difficult.

5. Get everyone to hold their smile in front of their mouth where everyone can see. Look around the circle.

6. Now ask everyone to turn their smile plate upside down. What happens to the smile? It turns into a sad face!

7. Stand up and dance around the room, turning the plate up and down as you say 'happy face', 'sad face', making your movements match the face on the plate.

I feel like a volcano
Managing anger

What you need:

- A picture storybook about being angry, such as *The Bad Tempered Ladybird* by Eric Carle (Puffin); *When Sophie Gets Angry, Really, Really Angry* by Molly Garrett Bang (Scholastic); *I Feel Angry* by Brian Moses (Wayland); *Where the Wild Things Are* by Maurice Sendak (Red Fox)

Preparation:

- Read your chosen storybook through so you know what happens.

Taking it forward

- Offer the children sticky notes to draw what makes them angry. Use these for discussions.

- Do some more movement sessions exploring strong feelings such as anger. Be a volcano, slowly building up to an explosion, then calming down again.

What's in it for the children?

This activity gives children practice in recognising the facial features of anger.

A story or two

I'm Feeling Angry by Lisa Regan (A&C Black)

Where the Wild Things Are by Maurice Sendak (Red Fox)

What to do:

1. Gather the children in a circle. Have the book ready.

2. Tell them that your story today is about being angry. Ask the children to think about being angry and what it does to your face and body. Make angry faces, get up and stamp around in an angry way. Talk about how it feels like you have a volcano inside you when you are angry.

3. Sit down again, and ask the children what you could do to stop yourself feeling angry. Accept all suggestions! If they need help in thinking, suggest deep breathing, counting to ten, thinking of something else.

4. Ask the children to think about these feelings as you read the story.

5. Read your chosen story right through without stopping.

6. Talk about the story. Why did the character get angry? What did they look like, what did they do? How did they calm down, what did they look like then?

7. End the session with 'pass a frown' and then 'pass a smile' around the circle.

36

50 fantastic ideas for exploring emotions

It just makes me mad!

Recognising what makes people angry

What you need:

- Some pictures of angry faces
- Flipchart or clipboard

Preparation:

- Try to be honest about your own feelings and what makes you cross. Make a list.

Taking it forward

- Write the list in a book, with one of the children's 'triggers' on each page. Let the children illustrate the book.

- Build the strategies into your daily routine, giving the children practice in taking control of their own behaviour.

What's in it for the children?

This activity gives children practice in recognising some of the triggers to anger.

A story or two

When Sophie Gets Angry, Really, Really Angry by Molly Garrett Bang (Scholastic)

Trumpet: The Little Elephant with a Big Temper by Jane Clarke (Simon & Schuster)

What to do:

1. Gather the children in a circle.

2. Ask them to remember a time when they were really angry. Some children will engage better with other words such as cross or mad.

3. Give them time to talk to each other about being angry, cross or mad.

4. Can you make a list together of the triggers that make children angry?

5. Let the children suggest as you list these triggers on a flipchart or clipboard.

6. Spread out the angry pictures you have found and ask the children to pick one to talk about. Why is this person angry? Can you tell the story?

7. Now ask them if they know what makes grown-ups angry. Share some of these, and ask why the children think this is so.

8. Go back to the children's list. Are any of the things the same? Are there things that make everyone angry?

9. Finally, share some ways to control anger – practise deep breathing or counting to ten.

Cool down corner
Strategies for controlling emotions

What you need:

- A range of comforting resources, such as blankets, cushions or beanbags
- A soft toy or teddy

Preparation:

- Put the resources somewhere easy to reach, but not in sight.
- Now think about your room and whether there are places for children to withdraw if they feel angry or are losing control.

What to do:

1. Gather the children in a circle.

2. Remind them that you are talking about feelings and how everyone can help if their friends are sad, cross or lonely.

3. Today you are going to talk about what to do if you feel cross or like a volcano. What does it feel like to have a volcano inside you? What makes you feel like this? (See also page 36).

4. Now ask the children what someone could do to cool down if they have a volcano growing inside them. Take all suggestions seriously.

5. One suggestion will probably be to distract yourself by doing something else or walking away.

6. Then you can say 'Where could you go if you were feeling like this?' Again take all suggestions seriously, discussing the positives and problems of each place.

7. Talk about places in your room and choose a 'cool down corner' together: it may be under a table, in a corner, outside, behind a cupboard.

8. Work together to decide how to make this a good and comfortable place to be. Show the children the resources and let them choose what to include.

Taking it forward

- Don't let the 'cool down corner' become a place of punishment – children can use it at any time to withdraw, even if they are not feeling cross but they just need some peace.

- Continue to add things to the 'cool down corner'; a light, a soft throw, a basket of books.

What's in it for the children?

This activity gives children practice in recognising and controlling their own feelings.

A story or two

Cool Down and Work Through Anger by Cheryl Meiners (Free Spirit)

Hands Are Not For Hitting by Martine Agassi (A&C Black)

Join the glitterati!

Managing feelings

What you need:

- Some empty water bottles
- Tubes of glitter glue and clear gel glue
- Coloured glitter
- A funnel
- Warm water
- Strong glue or duct tape

Preparation:

- Clean the labels and surface glue off the bottles and wash them thoroughly.

- Half-fill one bottle with warm water, add a small tube of glitter glue and some loose glitter. Experiment by adding more clear gel glue. This will make the glitter slow down.

- Top up with more warm water.

- Put on the lid and shake to mix.

- Secure the lid with strong glue or duct tape and test for leaks.

What to do:

1. Put the bottle in the middle of the carpet, covered with a cloth.

2. Gather the children in a circle.

3. Tell them that you have made something for the 'cool down corner' (see page 38) or for times when children are feeling upset.

4. Take the fabric off the bottle and ask the children what they think you have made.

5. Invite one of the children to gently shake the bottle and put it back on the floor. Suggest that the children should lie down so they can see what is happening in the bottle.

6. Ask the children how they feel when they are watching the bottle. They may need some help with suitable words to express how they feel.

7. Shake the bottle once more and watch as the glitter spins. Pass a smile round the circle as you watch.

Taking it forward

- Offer the resources for the children to make more bottles of different colours or with different glittery things inside, such as sequins, tinsel, lametta or water beads.

- Put the bottles in a basket in your 'cool down corner'.

What's in it for the children?

This activity gives children practice in managing their own emotions by using comfort objects.

A story or two

Calm Down Boris by Sam Lloyd (Templar Publishing)

Cool Down and Work Through Anger by Cheryl Meiners (Free Spirit)

50 fantastic ideas for exploring emotions

I'm OK, you're OK

Recognising personal emotions

What you need:

- A turn-taking object such as a shell or small soft toy.

What you need:

- Identify the things you like and fear, so you can start the game.

Taking it forward

- Use this game before you introduce a new activity or when you are going on a visit. It will give children a chance to share their worries and concerns.

- Help the children to make some OK/Not OK picture cards. You could use clip art.

What's in it for the children?

This activity gives children a non-threatening way to talk about their preferences and fears.

A story or two

The Tiger Who Came to Tea by Judith Kerr (HarperCollins)

Things I Like by Anthony Browne (Walker Books)

What to do:

1. Sit with the children in a circle.

2. Tell them you are going to learn another feelings game. This time it is about things you like and things you don't.

3. Talk about things that people like and things they dislike: spiders, chocolate, snakes, kittens, babies, monsters, superheroes. Make sure children understand that you can feel comfortable with something your friend is not comfortable with.

4. Start the game yourself with something like this 'I'm OK with cats, but I'm not OK with tigers'.

5. Turn to the child next to you, pass them the turn-taking object and say 'What are you OK with?' 'What are you not OK with?' Let them tell you, using 'I'm OK with... I'm not OK with ...'. It doesn't matter if they repeat what someone else has said.

6. Now pass the game on around the circle. If any child doesn't want to join in, they can just pass on the object. They must stay in the circle, but they don't have to speak.

7. Continue round the circle until everyone has had a chance to speak.

Scary scary!
Recognising and naming emotions

What you need:
- Dark fabrics
- Torches and other lights

Preparation:
- Make a dark place in your room by putting up a pop-up tent or hanging up some fabric. Put a light in this area so children are not too scared.

Taking it forward
- Make a display about 'What I can do if I'm scared'. Let the children draw pictures and add words themselves.
- Read *I'm Going on a Bear Hunt* by Michael Rosen (Walker) or watch a version from YouTube.

What's in it for the children?
This activity gives children practice in recognising and naming emotions.

A story or two
The Owl Who was Afraid of the Dark by Jill Tomlinson (Egmont)

The Gruffalo's Child by Julia Donaldson (Macmillan Children's Books)

What to do:
1. Sit together in the dark place you have made.
2. Ask the children if they like the dark. Tell them that everyone is scared sometimes, and it's OK to be scared.
3. Tell them about some of the things that grown-ups are scared of: mice, flying on planes, swimming, heights, bats, thunder, snakes etc. Explain that some of these things are really scary, some are not, but recognise that it's difficult to stop the feeling.
4. Ask the children to tell you about some of the things they are scared of. Don't ever force a child to talk, just respond to those who offer.
5. Play 'I'm OK, I'm not OK' about being scared. Start the game yourself: 'I'm OK about the dark, I'm not OK about bats'. Then pass the game along. Remember that it's fine if a child just passes when it's their turn.
6. Now talk about what you could do if you are feeling scared. The children may offer all sorts of ideas, and it's important to accept every idea. Jot them down if you can.

My first day
Being new

What you need:

- A book about starting school, such as **Starting School** by Janet Ahlberg (Puffin), **I'm Too Absolutely Small for School** (Charlie and Lola) by Lauren Child (Orchard), or **Do I Have to go to School?** by Lesley Harker (Wayland)

Preparation:

- Choose a story about starting school, or make one up, using a puppet or other character.
- Remind yourself of the feelings that children experience on their first day.

What to do:

1. Sit with the children and remind them that this is a time to think about feelings.

2. Tell the children that the story you are going to read is one about starting school. Can they remember how they felt when they started school or nursery?

3. Give them some time to talk to a partner about the feelings, then quickly go round the group with each child finishing the phrase – 'I felt ...'. Join in yourself.

4. Now show the children the book you have chosen and introduce it by telling them something about the story.

5. Read the book through without stopping, making sure everyone can see the pictures.

6. Talk about the feelings of the children in the story. Were they always happy, always scared? What did the adults do to make them feel better? What did the other children do?

7. Finally, take turns to think of something that would help the new children feel better by finish the phrase 'I would…'.

Taking it forward

- Visit your nursery class or the local playgroup to make friends with some younger children.

- Involve the children in making a Welcome Book for new children coming to your setting.

What's in it for the children?

This activity gives children practice in empathy, sharing feelings with others.

A story or two

Don't Eat the Teacher by Nick Ward (Scholastic)

How do Dinosaurs go to School? by Jane Yolen (HarperCollins)

Bear is lost!

Using stories to explore emotions

What you need:

- **A teddy**

Preparation:

- Think about the shape of the story and how you will keep it going.

Taking it forward

- Share experiences of being lost.
- Collect some simple objects in a story bag, and use this when you are making up stories together.

What's in it for the children?

This activity gives children practice in empathising through collaborative stories.

A story or two

Dogger by Shirley Hughes (Red Fox)

This is the Bear by Sarah Hayes (Walker)

What to do:

1. Sit with the children and hold the teddy bear on your lap.

2. Explain that you are going to make up a story about this bear. His name is Ted and he lives in a school. Pass the bear around so each child can hold it.

3. Tell the children that you will be making up the story together, and the children can decide what is going to happen.

4. Start the story yourself by saying 'This story is called 'The School Bear is Lost!'".

   Ted is taken on a class trip to the zoo.

5. When you have established the story line, pause and say 'What do you think happened next?' Children are good at taking part in storytelling, so all you have to do is make sure everyone who wants to contribute can!

6. During the story make sure you also ask, 'How do you think the children felt?' or 'How do you think Ted felt?' so you are still concentrating on emotions during the story.

7. This story may become long or short, depending on the contributions of individuals. If it is going on too long, you may have to intervene to draw it to a comfortable ending.

Oh, oh, the Gruffalo!

Being brave

What you need:

- **The story of *The Gruffalo*** **by Julia Donaldson** (Macmillan Children's Books)
- **Finger puppets of a mouse, a snake, a fox and the Gruffalo** (you can download these from Bookstart, www.bookstart.org.uk)

Preparation:

- Print, cut out and make one set of the Gruffalo finger puppets.
- Think about bravery, and how it makes you behave differently on the outside from how you feel on the inside.

Taking it forward

- Print some more finger puppet sheets so the children can make their own and play the story out.
- Watch the Gruffalo DVD, and talk about brave voices as well as brave faces.

What's in it for the children?

This activity gives children practice in recognising different emotions.

A story or two

The Tiger Who Came to Tea by Judith Kerr (HarperCollins)

Big, Brave Brian by M P Robertson (Frances Lincoln)

What to do:

1. Sit with the children and remind them that this is a time for thinking and talking about feelings. Today you are going to tell them a story about a very brave mouse.

2. Ask them if they know anyone who is really brave, and what sort of people need to be brave.

3. Now ask the children what the difference is between how you feel inside, and how you look on the outside when you are being brave. Share some of the children's memories of times when they have been brave.

4. Pass a brave face round the circle.

5. Now hold up the Gruffalo book. Ask the children if they know the story, and remind them that the mouse in the story is very brave.

6. Ask the children to help you tell the story. Some of them can use the finger puppets. Others can make 'feelings faces' as you read the story.

7. Read the story though as they listen, think and respond.

8. Now think about the times in the story when the mouse was brave, using the pictures in the book to help the discussion. Can you tell that the mouse is being brave by looking at the pictures?

My lovely mum

Exploring emotions, such as love for their mum or dad

What you need:

- Whiteboards and pens for each child

Preparation:

- This is a good preparatory activity for making Mother's day gifts and cards.

- Be aware of any child for whom this activity might be painful, and change the focus to another important adult.

Taking it forward

- Photocopy the boards as reminders for the children when they make Mother's day cards and gifts. Make sure you offer a variety of materials for these – some mums don't like pink or flowers!

- Make a display of books about mothers.

What's in it for the children?

This activity helps children to think about people they love.

A story or two

My Mum by Anthony Browne (Doubleday)

My Mum is Fantastic by Nick Butterworth (Walker Books)

What to do:

1. Sit together in a group, children can sit with talking or friendship partners if they wish.

2. Explain that it will be Mother's day soon and you are going to talk about mums and dads (or other adults), how they look after us and how they make us feel.

3. Ask, 'How does your mum make you feel?'.

4. Now ask the children to draw a picture of their mum on their whiteboard, trying to remember what sort of hair she has and what she likes to wear. Give them time to talk and to think about their own mum.

5. Around this picture, ask the children to draw some of the things their mum likes – encourage them to really think hard about what their own mum likes – try not to influence them, just support their own thoughts.

6. When they are ready they can talk about their mum with their friend or talk partner.

7. Go round the group taking turns to say 'My Mum likes …'

I can't do it – yet!

Talking about learning to do new things

What you need:

- Space for circle time

Preparation:

- Remind yourself of the tune to Frère Jacques

What to do:

1. Gather the children in a circle.

2. 'Let's think of all the things we can do that make us feel very clever and grown-up.'

3. Say that this is a new song for us all to sing – it sounds like Frère Jacques with different words.

   We can do it, we can do it,
   Yes we can, yes we can,
   We can do our coats up, we can do our coats up
   Yes we can, yes we can.

4. Sing the song again, choosing a child to suggest something else they can do.

5. Sing the song several times.

6. Now say, 'Sometimes we try to do something and we can't do it, and we feel really cross and upset. Can you remember what that's like? How does it feel? What does it make your face and body do?'

7. Invite some children to contribute experiences.

8. What should you do if you can't do something the first time you try it?

9. Take some suggestions from the children.

10. Encourage them to say 'I can't do that yet' instead of just 'I can't do that.'

Taking it forward

- Make a display of photos of the things the children can do. They could add words or short sentences starting with 'I can...'.

- Remind children that there are lots of things they will learn in their lives, and that everyone keeps on learning.

What's in it for the children?

This activity gives children practice in recognising that frustration can be part of learning new things.

A story or two

Giraffes Can't Dance by Giles Andreae (Orchard)

The Snail and the Whale by Julia Donaldson (Macmillan Children's Books)

You can't say 'you can't play'

Feeling left out

What you need:

- A puppet or doll

Preparation:

- Choose a name for the puppet/doll (the puppet in this version of the story is called Jarek).

- This activity is about feeling left out. Make up a simple story about your character being left out of a game by other children.

What to do:

1. Sit in a circle with talk partners, and put the doll or puppet on your knee.

2. Introduce the character and say that you have a story to tell about what happened to him/her at school/nursery one day.

3. Before you tell the story, ask the children if they have ever felt left out of a game. Let them talk to a talk partner before sharing some of their experiences.

4. Now tell your story. You could start like this:

'One day Jarek felt left out. He was in the garden at his school and he saw some of the children playing with the bikes. How do you think Jarek felt when he saw his friends?' Pause for comments.

'Jarek went over to his friends and asked them if he could play. The other children said 'No, you can't play with us, go away!' How do you think he felt now?'

'He said, please let me play, but the other children just rode away on their bikes and left him on his own. He began to feel very sad, and tears came into his eyes. He didn't know what to do.'

5. Ask the children what Jarek could do, and what they could do to help if their friend felt left out. Listen carefully to their suggestions. They may not all be ideal responses, but treat every child with respect, saying 'That's one thing he could do, good thinking.'

6. Continue the story, involving the children whenever you can,

'Well, this is what happened. Megan and Lucas looked through the window and saw Jarek crying. They tapped on the window and asked him to come and play in the home corner with them. His teacher saw what happened and at Group time, she talked to all the children about Jarek's problem, and asked for their help. The children thought about the problem and what do you think they decided to do?'

Pause.

7. The children at Jarek's school decided that they would say "You can't say 'you can't play" in their class, children should be kind and welcoming to each other.

Taking it forward

- Keep your puppet or doll as a thinking resource, and use it to explore situations and problems that arise in the group.

- Help the children to be assertive like those in the story.

What's in it for the children?

This activity gives children practice in being assertive.

A story or two

How to be a Friend by Laurene Krasny Brown (Little, Brown)

How to Catch a Star by Oliver Jeffers (HarperCollins)

Mystery friend
Describing others

What you need:

- **Photos of the children in the group.**

Preparation:

- If you don't have any photos, take some with a digital camera and print them (four to an A4 page is about the right size). Laminate them or stick them on card to make a set of photos for all sorts of games.

Taking it forward

- Leave the photo cards where the children can play games with them.

- Make another set of cards with self-portraits done with a mirror, or portraits of their friends.

What's in it for the children?

This activity gives children practice in describing people, their likes and dislikes.

A story or two

All Kinds of People by Emma Damon (Tango Books)

It's OK to be Different by Todd Parr (Little, Brown)

What to do:

1. Sit with the children in a circle.

2. Show them the photos and explain that you are going to play a guessing game called 'Can you guess who this is?'.

3. Say 'This is how you play – I'm going to pick a card and without showing it to you, I'm going to tell you about the person on the card, See if you can guess who it is'.

4. Pick a card and start to describe the child on it. Make it simple to start with, describing hair colour and length, gender, and something they like – for example – 'This person is a boy. He is very tall and he has brown hair. He loves making Lego models. Can you guess who it is?'

5. Now ask one volunteer to walk round the outside of the circle, pausing behind each child, saying 'Is it this one?, Is it this one?' and the other children say 'yes' or 'no' as they look at each one.

6. When the child has been identified, choose another card and play again. Once the children are used to the game, a child could sit by you to pick a photo and help you to describe the mystery child.

7. Play until the children have had enough or all the cards have been used.

50 fantastic ideas for exploring emotions

Slice!

Recognising individual features

What you need:

- **Photos of the children in the group**
- **Scissors** (a pair between two)

Preparation:

- If you don't have any photos, take some with a digital camera and print them out (four to an A4 page is about the right size).
- Cut the pictures into individual photos.

Taking it forward

- Offer some more photos so the children can play 'Slice!' again, maybe cutting the photos into more pieces.

- Stick all the pieces of the photos randomly onto a big piece of card and see if the children can spot themselves and their friends.

What's in it for the children?

Making a poem in this way gives children the confidence of working with a group in a non-threatening activity.

A story or two

Friends by Kim Lewis (Walker)

Frog and Toad are Friends by Arnold Lobel (HarperCollins)

What to do:

1. Sit the children in pairs in a circle.

2. Show the children the photos and explain that you are going to play another photo game called 'Slice!'

3. Say 'This is how you play – I'm going to give you each a photo of yourself. Look at the photos carefully, then swap with your friend and look at their photo. Talk about your faces.'

4. Give the photos out and leave the children to talk for a while.

5. Now give a pair of scissors to each pair of children, so they have to work together.

6. Show the children how to fold their pictures across the faces so the mouth is on one piece and the eyes on the other. Then they need to help each other to slice along the fold (younger children may need some adult help).

7. When the children have done this, ask them to put the four pieces on the floor and play with them, putting the two faces together in different ways, to see what they look like.

8. Talk about the way faces change with different eyes and different mouths.

Take that baby back!
Talking about feeling jealous

What you need:

- Photos of babies, or a baby doll
- A card with a girl's cross face on it (a photo or a simple drawing).

Preparation:

- Think about how to present this story.

What to do:

1. Bring the baby doll to the group, and introduce it to the children.

2. Talk about babies and how they make us feel. Most children will talk about warm feelings and how much they like babies.

3. Now show the children the picture of the child's face and say:

'We all love babies most of the time, but sometimes we may feel differently. This is Beth, and she sometimes wished that her mum and dad would take their new baby back to the place they got him from. She felt very sad and left out, and didn't want to share her mum and dad with the new baby. Sometimes she pretended she was a baby too, and cried, talked baby talk, or rolled on the floor! When Beth's mum told her to behave, she said she wished they didn't have a new baby, she didn't want him!'

4. Why do you think Beth felt like that? What do you think happened to make her feel that way?

5. Give the children some time to think and talk to each other. Then share some suggestions – remember to accept every contribution the children make, by saying 'Good thinking' or 'That's another idea.'

6. Share thoughts about the things babies do that get attention from parents, making older children feel left out.

7. Ask the children how they could help Beth to feel better about her new little brother.

Taking it forward

- Write some of the children's ideas on sticky notes and make a book or display called 'How to make friends with a baby'.

- Invite one of your families to bring a baby brother or sister to visit your group. Make sure you give the big brother or sister plenty of attention during and after the visit!

What's in it for the children?

This activity gives children practice in recognising feelings of jealousy.

A story or two

Peepo! Janet Ahlberg (Puffin)

I'm Important Too! Jen Green (Wayland)

50 fantastic ideas for exploring emotions

Throw your socks in the box!
Releasing frustration

What you need:

- Enough rolled pairs of socks (or beanbags) for each person
- An empty cardboard box

Preparation:

- Children often find it hard to remember the things that frustrate them. Keep a list in your planning folder of the things that frustrate children and make them lose their tempers.

- Remind yourself of the song 'We can do it' (page 47).

Taking it forward

- Decorate the box with lots of photos of children's faces, and let anyone who is frustrated throw all the socks in the box to get rid of the feeling.

- Remember to talk about things the children can't do yet, and play the game again.

What's in it for the children?

This activity gives children practice in adjusting to feelings of frustration.

The Huge Bag of Worries by Virginia Ironside (Hodder)

Titch by Pat Hutchins (Red Fox)

What to do:

1. Sit with the children and put the box in the middle. Say 'Today we are going to play 'Throw your socks in the box".

2. If you have already explored what they can do and can't do yet, remind them of the song 'We can do it,' and sing it together.

3. Say that today you are going to talk about how you feel when you can't do things.

4. Ask all the children if they can make their face show how they feel when they can't do something.

5. Now give each child a rolled up pair of socks and show them how to play.

6. Start yourself, saying something like, 'I can drive a car but I can't play the piano – yet!' and throw your socks in the box.

7. Ask for volunteers to talk about something they can do, and something they can't do yet.

8. The first time you play this, don't insist that every child contributes. When all the volunteers have had a go, sing the song again and at the end changing the words to 'We can play 'Socks in a box, but we can't fly an aeroplane/go to the moon/ride a bike – yet!' as you throw the last pairs of socks in the box.

50 fantastic ideas for exploring emotions

Finger fun

Recognising contrasting emotions

What you need:

- **Small round stickers** (two per child)
- **Fine felt pen**

Taking it forward

- Sing the song at group times so the children can use it during storytelling.

- Use a stamp pad to make some fingerprints. Turn these into pictures by adding expressions to each print.

What's in it for the children?

This activity helps children to name and talk about a range of feelings.

A story or two

Are You Sad Little Bear? Rachel Rivett (Lion Hudson)

The Giving Tree Shel Silverstein (Particular Books)

What to do:

1. Sit with the children and make sure they can all see your face.

2. Get the children to hold up the index (first) fingers of both hands. Put a happy sticker on one finger and a sad sticker on the other.

3. Explain that you are going to play another feelings game and learn another feelings song.

4. This is the song. It sounds like the 'Hokey Cokey' with different words. Sing the song a couple of times. The children hold up their first fingers, one for happy, one for sad:

   You put your happy finger in
   You put your happy finger out
   In, out, in, out
   Shake it all about
   And put it in your lap.

   You put your sad finger in
   You put your sad finger out
   In, out, in, out
   Shake it all about
   And put it in your lap.

5. When the children have practised a bit, sing the song again, then tell a little story with sad and happy events, maybe something that has happened recently in the group. The children hold up their fingers to reflect the emotions.

Fish for a feeling

Recognising and naming emotions from expressions

What you need:

- Some table tennis balls
- Permanent marker
- An aquarium net or slotted spoon
- A water tray
- Food colouring (optional)
- Plastic sheet

Preparation:

- Draw feelings faces on the balls with a permanent marker (happy, sad etc).
- Put the water tray on the plastic sheet on the floor, and fill with enough water for the balls to float easily. Add some food colouring.
- Put the balls in a basket or bowl.

What to do:

1. Gather the children round the water tray. If they can sit on the floor it will be easier.

2. Introduce the game 'This is another feelings game, called Fish for a feeling'. Show the children the balls. Pass them round so the children can see the different feelings faces.

3. Let the children drop the balls in the water.

4. Invite one child to fish one of the balls out with the slotted spoon. When they have done this, ask everyone to make the face.

5. Say 'Can you think of a time when you felt like this?'.

6. Share experiences, before returning the ball to the water.

7. Continue the game.

8. While you play you could sing this song:

   One, two, three, four, five
   Feelings fishes all alive
   Quickly catch one of you can
   Make the face and fish again.

Taking it forward

- Give the children some more balls to make their own feeling faces to fish for.

What's in it for the children?

This activity gives children practice in naming emotions from facial expressions.

A story or two

The Fish Who Could Wish by John Bush (Oxford University Press)

Fidgety Fish by Ruth Galloway (Little Tiger Press)

Our new friend

Making friends and finding out about new people

What you need:

- **A large puppet, or a doll** (the character should be new to the children)
- **A blank book**

Preparation:

- This activity is about introducing a new character in your room. Set aside time to incorporate the character gradually over several sessions.
- Practise holding the doll so you can talk about it in a relaxed way, and start to think about the character and their history.

Taking it forward

- Make sure Carlo has a special place to sit during the day. The children should be able to see him all the time.
- Bring Carlo to group times, particularly when you are talking about feelings. Include him as a character when you want to talk about emotional situations.

What's in it for the children?

This activity gives children practice in empathising.

A story or two

My New Friend by Jillian Powell (Wayland)

Moving Molly by Shirley Hughes (Red Fox)

What to do:

1. Gather the children in a circle, and sit the puppet or doll on your knee.

2. Explain that you have brought a new friend to the group, and you would like to tell them something about him.

3. 'This is Carlo. He has just moved here and he is going to be in our class. He has curly black hair and blue eyes, and he is five.'

4. Pass Carlo round the circle, so everyone can hold him.

5. When he gets back to you, tell the children that they can ask questions to find out more about him. Make sure you note these down so you don't get muddled later.

6. Sing a welcome song to him:

   Welcome Carlo, welcome Carlo
   We are pleased to meet you
   Welcome Carlo, welcome Carlo
   We hope you like us too.

7. Finally, ask for volunteers to look after Carlo during his first day.

I can't wait!

Recognising emotions, excitement

What you need:

- A boy doll or puppet

Preparation:

- Read through the story so you know what's coming.

What to do:

1. Sit with the children in a group and the doll or puppet on your knee. Introduce the character and give him a name, we have called ours Glenn.

2. Tell the children that today's feelings story is all about Glenn and the football match.

3. Ask whether any of the children has ever been to a football match. If so, let them tell the group about how they felt before the match.

4. Now tell the story – 'This is what happened to Glenn:'

On **Monday** his dad said 'Do you want to go to the match on Saturday Glenn?'

Glenn was so excited that he nearly burst. He had never been to a match before! 'Yes!!' he said 'I do!'

Glenn's mum said, 'Don't get too excited, you've got four more days to wait.

But on **Tuesday** Glenn was so excited, he bounced on his bed till he fell off on the floor. His mum said, 'Calm down Glenn!' so he made a model of a football ground and he felt a bit better.

On **Wednesday** Glenn was so excited, he kicked a football into his friend Morton. His teacher said, 'Calm down Glenn!' so he counted to ten, wrote a 'sorry' note to Morton and felt a bit better.

On **Thursday** Glenn was so excited, he jumped on the settee and knocked his mum's plant off the table. His dad said, 'Calm down Glenn!' so he helped to clear up the mess and put the plant back in the pot and he felt a bit better.

On **Friday** Glenn was so excited, he couldn't go to sleep at bedtime. 'Calm down Glenn, or you won't go to the match!' said his mum. Glenn thought he would burst! His mum came and read him his favourite story and at last he went to sleep.

On **Saturday** Glenn put on his football kit as soon as he woke up. His dad took him to the football match and they had a great time. When Glenn got home he said to his mum, 'I'm sorry I got so excited, but I couldn't help it! Can I go again next week?'

5. Ask the children if they could remember what Glenn did to stop himself from being so excited. Can they remember being excited like Glenn? How did they cope with this feeling?

50 fantastic ideas for exploring emotions

Taking it forward

- Talk about exciting times and mark some events on a calendar or diary.

- Children need things to look forward to. Try to find something to look forward to every week, so children can get excited and learn ways to manage this.

What's in it for the children?

This activity gives children practice in managing their feelings.

A story or two

Not Now Bernard by David McKee (Andersen)

Big Day Out by Jess Stockham (Child's Play)

I'm sorry

Coping with problems

What you need:

- **A puppet** (the one used in 'Our new friend page 57 would be perfect)

Preparation:

- Practise the story below, or make up your own, using incidents from your setting.

What to do:

1. Gather the children in a circle, and sit the puppet on your knee.

2. Remind the children about Carlo (or the puppet you have named).

3. Say, 'Carlo's got a problem and he wants you to help him. Will you think about the problem and try to help?'

'Last week Carlo was playing with some of the children outside and they had made a really good den under the climbing fame. They used some old sheets and they had been working for a long time to fix them. Carlo and his friends were just sitting in the den having a pretend picnic, when some of the other children ran past and pulled all the sheets down. They laughed at Carlo and his friends and said that making dens was a baby game. They grabbed the sheets and took them to the top of the climbing frame.

Carlo and his friends were very sad. They didn't know what to do. What do you think they should do?'

4. Wait for suggestions. Treat all suggestions with respect, praising the children for thinking and having ideas.

'Well, Carlo and his friends did go and tell the grown-ups. Their teacher came and told the others to come down from the climbing frame.

When they did, what do you think the teacher asked them to do?'

5. Invite the children to make suggestions. Discuss the options, and then say:

'The children did say they were sorry, and they did help Carlo and his friends to build their den again. But later, one of the girls said Carlo was a tell-tale, and that upset him very much.

What could Carlo do to try to solve the problem before fetching the grown-ups?'

6. Invite the children to offer ideas.

7. Make sure Carlo thanks the children for their help.

Taking it forward

- Following this session, if difficulties arise, remind children gently about the strategies they suggested for solving problems and being assertive.

- Encourage children to try solving their own problems before coming to an adult but never let them feel that you have abandoned them.

What's in it for the children?

This activity gives children practice in developing their own strategies to solve problems.

A story or two

Sorry by Norbert Landa (Little Tiger Press)

Words Are Not for Hurting by Elizabeth Verdick (A&C Black)

Superhero sadness

Being sensitive to others' feelings

What you need:

- Some superhero figures
- A puppet or doll

Preparation:

- Practise the story so you can tell it without the book, as you will need to hold the puppet.

What to do:

1. Sit with the children, with the puppet or doll on your knee. Put the superhero figures somewhere nearby.

2. Introduce the character and give it a name (we have chosen to use a girl doll, called Sam).

3. Tell the children that Sam has a problem and she wants their help. This is the problem:

'Yesterday, Sam wanted to play with the superhero figures. She got them out and was sitting on the floor, ready to play when some other children came over and said, 'You can't play with superheroes, they are boys' toys. They said that Sam was a boy's name too, so she must be a boy. They laughed and ran away.

Sam felt sad and a bit cross. She wasn't a boy! But she really did want to play with the superhero toys. What could she do?'

4. Encourage the children to talk to each other about Sam's problem, then share thoughts about how Sam felt and what she could do. Remember that every child's solution to a problem should be treated with respect. Say 'Good thinking,' or 'Yes, she could do that.'

5. When everyone has contributed, or you think you have plenty of ideas, ask Sam what she thinks. Say something like 'Sam says thank you for all the ideas. She thinks that next time she feels upset, she will tell the other children that the toys are for everyone, and she can play with any of them. Then she's going to find someone else who wants to play with superheroes too.'

50 fantastic ideas for exploring emotions

Taking it forward

- Make sure children know that all the toys are for everyone to play with. Try not to give messages about which toys are for boys and which are for girls.

- Use characters from popular culture, including superheroes when you tell stories or use small world figures for focus activities.

What's in it for the children?

This activity gives children practice in being sensitive to the feelings of others.

A story or two

Super Daisy by Kes Gray (Red Fox)

Superhero School by Aaron Reynolds (Bloomsbury)

Hooray for happiness!

Enjoying being happy

What you need:

- An old sheet or plain white fabric
- Chunky felt pens
- Duct tape or masking tape

Taking it forward

- Make small flags or streamers and have a happy parade round your school or setting, make everyone smile!

- Collect objects and pictures of things in happy colours.

What's in it for the children?

This activity gives children practice in recognising that they can contribute to the happiness of others.

A story or two

Mrs Rainbow by Neil Griffiths (Red Robin Books)

Sometimes I Feel Sunny by Gillian Shields (Picture Corgi)

What to do:

1. Gather the children in a circle near the sheet pieces.

2. Remind them that you are thinking about feelings, and today you are going to think about how to make people happy.

3. Ask the children 'What are the things that make us happy? What are the colours that make us feel happy?'

4. Go round the circle and ask, 'What makes you happy?' Remember that some children find it difficult to think of ideas, and may either copy another child or say nothing.

5. Now show the children the resources and say that you are going to make some big flags to cheer everyone up. They can all help to make the 'happy flags', by drawing things to make people feel happy.

6. Try not to direct the activity too much. Just gently remind them that the flags are 'happy flags'.

7. When the children have finished their drawings, they can write their names anywhere on their flag.

8. Ask the children where they think the flags should go, so they can cheer everyone up.